ıassenon
an Baths

Aerial view of the archaeological site at Chassenon with Longeas Roman baths in the foreground and a section of aqueduct in the hedge on the left. The remains of *"Montélu"* temple can be seen in the middle of the photo whilst on the right, covered by an overgrown area on the other side of the road, lies the *"Léna"* amphitheatre.

The Roman baths at Longeas, a small hamlet just outside Chassenon in Charente, are amongst the best preserved buildings of their type in the territory of Ancient Gaul, and possibly in the whole of what once was the Roman Empire. Classed as historical buildings in 1987 and owned by Charente Council since 1985, the extensive site open to visitors includes in fact only a small portion of the shrine and numerous buildings that once made up the large Gallo-Roman town of *Cassinomagus*. Archaeological remains still lie scattered in neighbouring fields and under the present day village of Chassenon, awaiting excavation.

From *Cassinomagus* to Chassenon

The Site and its Location

Chassenon is situated on a plateau bordered to the north by the River Vienne and to the south by one of the latter's affluents, the River Grène. It is located on the dividing line between the Charente and Haute-Vienne districts in an area called the Charente-Limousine, relatively distant from any major routes and roads, a situation that is markedly different from that in Roman times.

Site viewed from the north-east in 2004.

The town grew from an Imperial posting station (*mansio*) into a flourishing and attractive city in the province of Aquitania and is duly recorded in Peutinger's Table*. Under Roman rule, *Cassinomagus* (Chassenon) was located at the extreme Western edge of a district governed administratively from *Augustoritum* (modern-day Limoges), the main town of the Celtic Lemovices tribe. Even at its beginnings therefore, Chassenon lay on the borders of several tribal and subsequently Roman districts; lands of the Santones (Saintes) and Ecolisna (Iculisma or modern-day

Angoulême) tribes to the West, Pictones (Poitiers) to the North-West and Petrocorti (Périgueux) to the south. The fact that *Cassinomagus* was situated at a major crossroads between Agrippa's highway running East-West from Lyon to Saintes, and the North-South Poitiers-Périgueux Roman road, no doubt must have encouraged its growth. Also being

Roman Aquitania

The Romans divided Gaul into three large provinces: Aquitania, Celtica and Belgica. Each province was subdivided into autonomous regions *(civitates)*, these divisions later forming a model for church dioceses before becoming the basis of current *"départements"* or administrative areas in France today. Each *civitas* had a central city *(oppidum)*, a sort of local capital that governed the often large surrounding areas *(ager)*, consisting of rural or semi-urban towns and villages where a proportion of the population lived. These so-called secondary settlements were sometimes larger than their governing city but lacked any form of genuine administative or political independance. They were controlled by magistrates from the *civitas* capital; secondary settlements in Poitou-Charente included Naintré, Vendeuvre, Sanxay, Saint-Cybardeaux, Angoulême and Barzan as well as Chassenon itself.

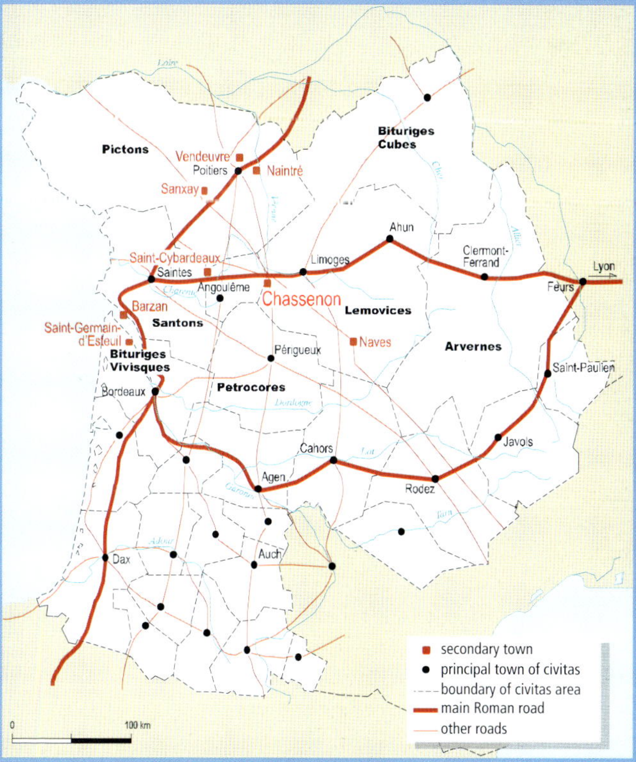

located a few hundred meters from the Vienne River which may have been navigable at the time, was probably an added factor favouring its development.

Landscape and Environment

Geologically speaking, Chassenon is in a distinctive area characterised by metamorphic rocks known as impact breccia* caused by a meteorite that collided with the Earth at this spot in the late Triassic Age, approximately 200 million years ago. The actual centre of the impact crater covers a zone of countryside stretching between the towns of Rochechouart and Chassenon and although the meteorite was not directly connected with the founding of Chassenon at this particular geographical location, it nevertheless provided ancient and modern builders alike with an original type of construction material. Quarries to extract the rock can still be seen in woods just South of Longeas hamlet.

Baths viewed from the north-west.

From an environmental point of view, the north-western fringes of the *Massif Central* area form an undulating zone made up of cold, wet flatlands, ideal for animal husbandry and forestry. Indeed,

"Great Wall", seen from the east (by entrance to Chassenon site).

Northern esplanade, with part of north gallery and rainwater drainage channel viewed from first floor on the east.

today, both landscape and local economy are dominated by a thriving lumber industry, principally exploiting forests of oaks, chestnut and alder trees, as well as a few relatively recent pine plantations. Analysis of charcoal (anthracology) and pollen (palynology) during excavation of the Chassenon baths established that in Roman times the area was very similar, being heavily wooded with oaks and beeches plus ash, willow, alder and several varieties of fruit trees. On the other hand, chestnut trees were rare before the 4th century AD. Seed analysis (carpology) has shown that crops cultivated here included grape vines, rye, wheat, corn for starch, millet, barley, oats and flax or possibly field beans.

General History

Nothing is known of the proto-historical site around Chassenon. Indeed, conjecture about a Gallic settlement or even an indigenous pre-Roman shrine lacks proof of any kind. All evidence so far however suggests that *Cassinomagus* and its shrine were built roughly seventy years after the Roman conquest, during the second half of the 1st century AD. Towards the end of the Flavian Dynasty (late 1st century AD) the settlement underwent a period of economic and municipal development that was to last throughout the High-Empire, from the 1st to 3rd century. Subsequent transformations in provincial administration as well as in political and religious life caused a downturn in the town's fortunes at the start of the 4th century. Nearby Angoulême for example obtained independence at that time and a few generations later the Visigoths were to settle in the western part of the province of Aquitania.

Statue of a cross-legged Gallo-Roman god, discovered in one of the town wells.

Although the baths and shrine seem to have been definitively abandoned between the 5th and 6th centuries, the town itself continued to exist, coming under the jurisdiction of the diocese of Limoges. A Royal Decree signed there in the 9th century and official records attesting to its status as the principal town of its "*viguery*"* or borough in the 10th century, provide sufficient evidence that *Cassinomagus* must have still retained a certain amount of power right through the Early Middle Ages.

Even though little is known concerning the town during the Middle Ages and early modern era, it seems that nearby Rochechouart and Chabanais gained in importance as Chassenon's influence declined, the town soon dwindling to a mere huddle of houses clustered around the parish church of Saint John the

Eglise Saint Jean-Baptiste (Church of Saint John the Baptist); detail of west front with early medieval crucifixion scene and re-use of Roman building materials.

Baptist. The latter was built in a clearly "archaic" style that almost certainly predates the 12th century.
Sarcophagi made from impact breccia* stone, found in the vicinity of the cemetery, prove that little changed over this period and Cassini's maps drawn up the 18th century depict Chassenon virtually as it is today.

Roman milestone used as Christian gravestone in Chassenon cemetery.

Roman Town and Shrine

Cassinomagus, which possibly means "oak market", was not a simple rural shrine, but a medium to large-sized town, traces of which have been found over an area of almost 300 hectares (740 acres). Such an apparently impressive scale of urban development must however be treated with caution since the town never occupied the whole site at any one period of time. The main nucleus of dwellings lies to the west of the present town at Lachenaud, Coutis and Acaccias, as well as under modern Chassenon itself. Excavation has uncovered the remains of houses plus a number of public edifices and also numerous wells, many of which

Map of *Cassinomagus* Shrine.

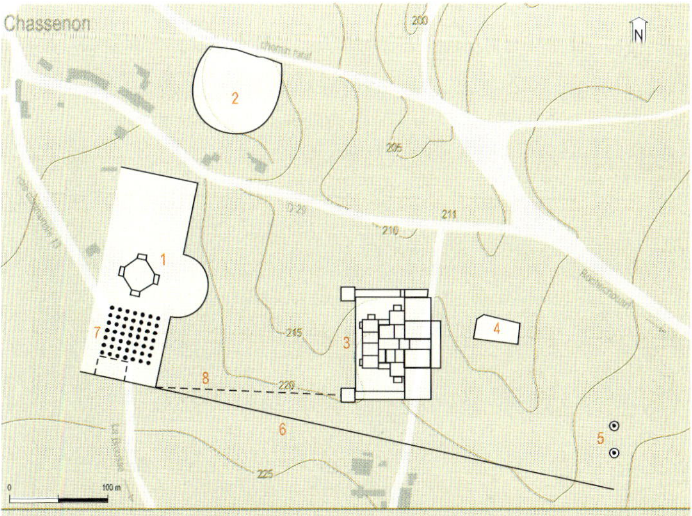

Layout of Roman buildings at Chassenon
1 temple
2 theatre-arena
3 public baths (*thermae*)
4 pool
5 small temples
6 aqueduct
7 cisterns and possible water tower
8 water supply channel to baths complex

were probably ceremonial. A large group of dwellings was located to the west of Longeas in 2003 as a result of electromagnetic surveys*.

But the centre of interest in *Cassinomagus* in Roman times was undoubtedly its large shrine situated to the south-east of the town and occupying an area of approximately 25 hectares (60 acres). This immense monumental complex was organized around its most significant building, a large temple, located to the west at Montélu. Its octagonal *cella**, was constructed on a *podium* on top of a natural hillock or mound that forms the highest point (222 m) of the shrine and surrounding town. A 200-m long esplanade bordered the temple which was dedicated to a deity whose identity has not yet been established. Running around the *cella* was a portico gallery (or *pteron*) with a semicircular *exhedra** on its eastern side. The southern half of the temple esplanade was occupied by a grid-like arrangement of at least forty-nine

"Montélu" Temple; plan based on excavations by J. - H. Moreau.

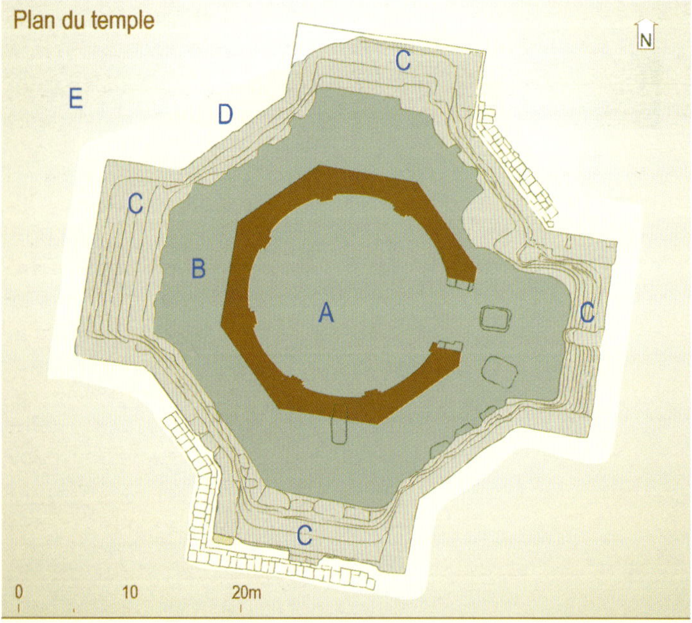

A *cella*
B gallery
C steps
D esplanade (excavated portions)
E unexcavated areas

cisterns, designed to stock water required for the baths. The temple has been excavated several times since the 19th century and was finally given the status of a protected historical monument in 1987. It is currently buried under a layer of soil, and therefore cannot be visited. A short distance away to the east, two small polygonal temples mark the eastern edge of the shrine in a small wood at Ville des Tempes. Although they are impossible to visit at the moment, we know from excavations of one of the them carried out in 1858 that the structure consisted of a central *fanum**-type temple with ten- or eight-sided *cella** and peripheral porticoed gallery.

Remains of *"Léna"* ancient Roman theatre in 1934.

The remains of a theatre were discovered in 1848 to the north of the shrine at La Léna near the modern westbound exit from Chassenon. Used as a quarry from 1913 onwards, the site continued to be degraded until classed as a historic monument in 1936 by which time it was in a rather poor state. Estimated as 70 metres in width with an unusual flattened semi-circular shape, the theatre also probably served as an arena or amphitheatre, so providing both entertainment and sport as well as additional religious functions connected with worship at the temples.

No major constructions appear to have been built on the large sweep of land that

Aerial view of the bath buildings in the 1960s, before roofing was installed.

forms a natural dip between the central temple at Montélu and the Chassenon bath complex at Longeas (described in detail below). Only a rectilinear masonry structure, currently hidden below ground, runs between the two areas. This might have served as the main channel feeding water from the cisterns to the baths. On the Eastern side, between the baths and two smaller temples, a natural slope leads to a stone-walled structure identified by aerial photography as an ornamental lake or pond.
Finally, to the south of the baths can be seen portions of a long wall built in *opus caementicium** that runs for one kilometre in an easterly direction. The structure is 2.15 m wide and undoubtedly was part of the aqueduct supplying water to the whole of *Cassinomagus*. Another section found in woods to the east suggests that perhaps water may have been extracted from springs at Londeix.

Northern gallery, south side seen from courtyard.

"Great Wall" on the east side of the baths, with reference mark showing soil level in 1958 before excavations began.

Excavating the Site

Despite its progressive abandonment over time, the Chassenon site has long fascinated historians. Preliminary excavations in the mid-19th century were carried out by J-H. Michon, A. Arbellot, A. Précigou and A. Masfrand, followed by F. Delage, P. Masfrand and P. Barrière, who confirmed the importance and scale of the Roman ruins. A significant number of wells in the vicinity were drained and investigated, and land around Montélu temple thoroughly surveyed. The Roman theatre was discovered at this time and quarrying of its stones commenced.
However the first extensive studies of the Chassenon baths and temple complex only really began in the 1950s with archaeological digs by members of the "Société des amis de Chassenon" under their president J.-H. Moreau, a resident of nearby Rochechouart. Moreau devoted over thirty years to rediscovering *Cassinomagus* and it is largely through his efforts that the baths at Longeas slowly came to light over the years between 1958 and 1988.

Initial excavations in the fifties.

As contemporary photographs show, the site known locally as the "Les caves de Longeas" (Longeas cellars) was nothing more than a wooded mound with no easy entry point, a favourite place for children to hide and play games. Since then a great many hands have been employed to make the site what it is today.

Under their chairman, Father J.-M Lecompte, the Friends of Chassenon Society continued to improve access and maintain upkeep of the site - for example constructing roofs to protect unearthed structures. Active excavations began again in 1995 with dozens of students spending several weeks every summer working on uncovering the ruins, and since 2000, Charente council has provided funds to further improve Chassenon for visitors and as a cultural heritage site.

View of the site from north-west in 1958 (left) and in 1978 (right).

Excavating the covered north *palaestra* in 2003.

Chassenon Baths: The Stamp of Imperial Rome in Charente

History of the Longeas Roman Baths at Chassenon

The history of the site is long and complex. Initial construction work began in the first half of the 1st century AD but it was only towards the end of the century, whilst Rome was under the Flavian Dynasty, that the Chassenon *thermae* were actually built. Several further generations were required to add lateral galleries and pools on the eastern side of the complex to complete the final layout of buildings. Thus the Roman baths that visitors can explore today reflect a structure that existed during the 2nd and 3rd centuries AD.

Towards the end of the 3rd century, diminishing affluence meant that the baths were less well maintained and a fire broke out, probably accidentally, destroying the whole edifice. The baths must have been such a vital component of *Cassinomagus* shrine that despite the scale of the operation, they were rapidly rebuilt and throughout the 4th century continued attracting bathers and the sick seeking a cure. The buildings however were not as luxurious as previously; most of the *hypocausts** were never repaired and expensive wooden floors were replaced by cheaper sand and earth coverings.

Relieving arch of the central sewer with bath buildings in the background, viewed from north gallery.

But the large hot water pools which had made *Cassinomagus* so famous still functioned as before.

All this stopped suddenly in the early years of the 5th century. The Roman baths seem to have been modified and used as a series of rural constructions from that time on, sheltering a small village within their ancient walls.

Excavations in the Eastern half of the baths revealed the existence of two houses occupying 100 m^2, each linked to a 70 m^2 hayloft or storage space in which traces of harvested and sorted plants were found, including rye, wheat, millet, barley, oats, and flax. The storage spaces were organised around several hearths used for drying and roasting the cereals and perhaps preparing gruel, cakes or bread. One or more grinding stones were found in the middle of these spaces not far away from a collection of small bells. A loaf of bread, 19 cm in diameter and 6 cm high, decorated with millet seeds, was found in one of four rooms that made up a neighbouring habitation and nearby a ball of linen thread suggests that weaving was carried out by the inhabitants of these dwellings. A shack abutting against the entrance was found to contain small bags of seeds and a selection of tools used by peasants at that time, such as a pick, hoe, gouges and knives.

When fire struck again in the late 5th century, the above houses were reconstructed using more expensive and stronger materials. During excavations,

Fifth century artefacts from public floor of the baths. Above; burnt loaf of bread discovered in 1998. Opposite; antique fake gold coin, small bell and iron pickaxe head.

Central corridor on ground floor with paving stones covering drainage channel.

a gold coin was found in the ashes of a hearth used to heat the main room of one of the houses, but upon closer examination it turned out to be an antique fake of a *tremessis* coin minted under the Visigoth emperor Majorian (AD 457-461). Under its gold surface, the coin was made of copper and bronze. Shortly before AD 550 the occupants seem to have inexplicably abandoned their homes in the former Roman baths, so ending five centuries of activity at Longeas. The forgotten site, undisturbed, slowly disappeared under layers of earth until archaeologists began investigating the area in the 19th and 20th centuries.

An Example of Ancient Roman Architecture

The remarkable state of preservation of the Longeas Baths at Chassenon provides us with an excellent example of Ancient Roman architecture.

Their construction must have required an impressive-sized workforce engaged for several months or even years. Having chosen an appropriate site, the ground first had to be prepared, taking advantage of the natural slope that drops six metres from south to north across the site. Workmen then had to dig out a large rectangle measuring 60 by 50 m to a depth of several metres in the clay soil so that the building's foundations could sit on a solid rock base.

Frigidarium and *caldarium* viewed from north esplanade.

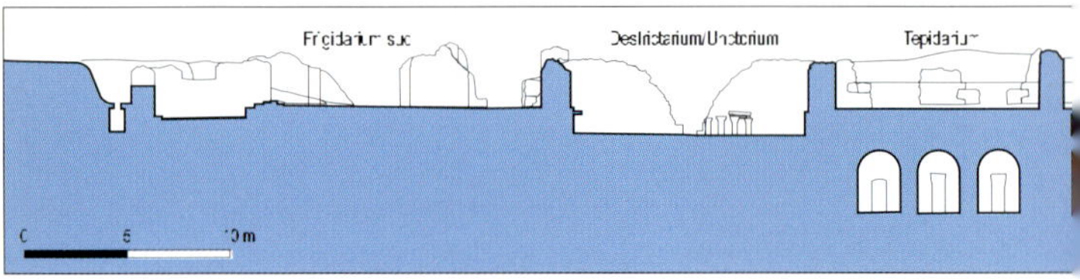

Transverse section along axis AB (cf. plan on inside cover) showing barrel-vaulted substructure spaces supporting floors on the level above (first floor).

The outer walls of the bath complex were then erected along the perimeter of the rectangle, not as single walls but doubled on the inside by a series of narrow vaulted basement rooms for added strength and designed to support the groundfloor above, used by the public. Though costly, this ingenious system enabled the public floor to be brought level with higher ground to the south and east, thus countering the site's slope.

Barrel-vaulted space under north *frigidarium*.

Technically speaking, construction of virtually all the walls and vaulting in the bathing complex involved the use of *opus caementicium**, a Roman form of concrete made from a slurry of lime mortar and stone. You will notice on your visit that very few large stones were

Transverse section along axis XY (see plan on inside cover) showing furnace yards and ash storage chambers (under *tepidarium*).

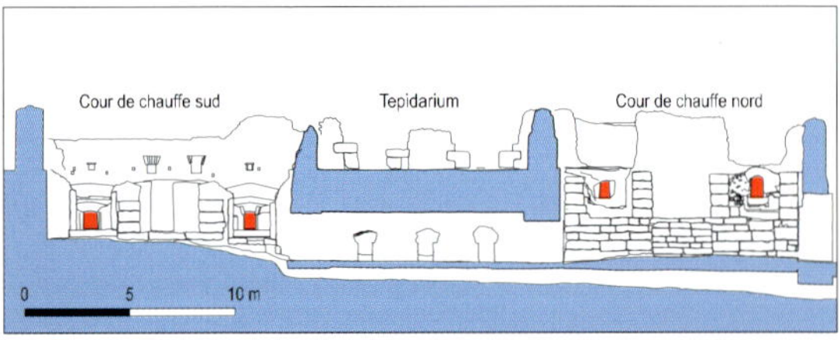

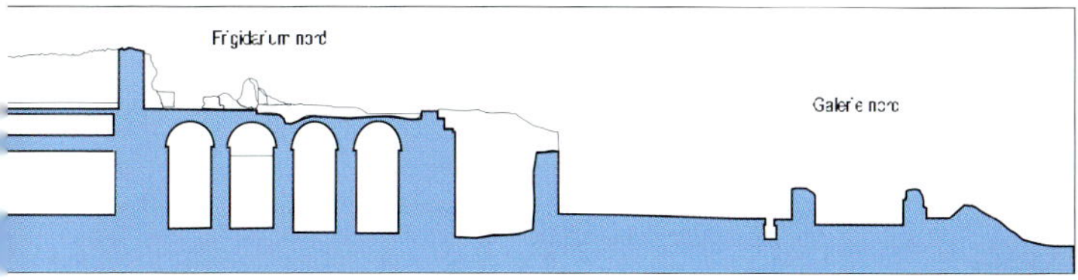

North façade with putlog-holes and *opus vittatum mixtum* wall facing.

Ash storage chamber; imprint of planking used in formwork on the vault is still visible.

employed as facings for walls in the building, the Roman architects preferring smaller 10 to 12 cm high blocks known as *opus vittatum**. When a course of large bricks was inserted into such a wall, as shown opposite, the technique was known as *opus vittatum mixtum**.

The Romans used concrete as a structural material to cover large spaces or as vaults. Arched wooden forms were made into which the concrete was poured and allowed to set before removal of the shuttering planks whose prints can still clearly be seen on the vaults of basement rooms in the Chassenon baths. Concrete ceilings had the added advantage of insulating heated rooms but sometimes traditional timber-frame roofs were used instead, as is the case in the *frigidaria**, *palaestra** and lateral galleries here, despite their large size. They consisted of square beams, 20-30 cm in width, made out of split heartwood from oaks with smaller sections in beech. The heavy frames needed to be strong for they not only had to carry large roof tiles jointed with mortar but also had to support the weight of a false ceiling hanging down from iron hooks.

Unlike many other Roman baths, no sign of mosaic decorations could be found at the Longeas site. Public spaces and pools were almost all finished with limestone flags quarried locally.

Evidence of wooden flooring was detected in at least two covered areas of the baths - the north-eastern *palaestra** used for sport and the southern gallery which served as a public passageway. The gallery floor for example was made

South hot-water pool lined with limestone paving and impressions of missing tiles on the pool floor.

from split planks of ash, appreciated for their suppleness and elasticity. As in all other Roman baths, rooms were equipped with a *hypocaust** system, litterally heating floors from below. A total of seventeen such rooms have been identified at Chassenon.
A clear view of the hypocaust system can be seen in the southern *destrictarium**/ *unctorium** and *caldarium** rooms. Essentially, concrete floors repose on an array of brick pillars (*pilae**), collectively known as a *suspensura**. The underfloor open space thus created enabled air heated in an outside furnace (*praefurnium**) to circulate, efficiently rise up the walls through inner hollow terra cotta bricks called *tubuli** and finally be evacuated from the building through vents or chimneys around the edges of the roof. Walls and floors were thus kept warm, fully insulated from the cold and no condensation formed on inside surfaces.

South *destrictarium / unctorium* chamber showing *pilae* brick columns designed to support the concrete floor above the hypocaust.

South *destrictarium/unctorium*; detail of hypocaust *pilae*.

Heated hall with remains of *tubuli* hot-air conduits forming the double-layered wall.

Fragment of mortar from bath walls painted red and white.

Contrary to accepted ideas, interior decoration of the rooms was lavish and varied. We know hard limestone facings were applied to the lower sections of walls in several rooms at Chassenon but elsewhere protection and decoration of walls largely involved paintwork, frequently coloured red, green and white. Stucco or marble sculptures further adorned the walls. Exterior facades of the bath buildings were coated in a red-coloured mortar.

Cleanliness, Luxury and Roman Civilisation

Public Roman baths or *thermae* were part of the Roman way of life; a place to meet friends, keep clean and sometimes be cured of ailments. The buildings that housed them in Ancient Gaul can be admired as impressive symbols of Roman civilisation, though in fact they are the direct descendants of an Ancient Greek idea that developed in the 4th century BC, that of providing warm baths in sports halls or gymnasiums. This then developed into a system whereby hot air from furnaces was channelled through galleries running under stone floors to heat rooms. Known as the hypocaust* system, it spread throughout Italy, made fashionable by a certain Sergius Orata of Campania in the 1st century BC and from there reaching other countries as the Roman Empire expanded.

Chassenon is a clear example of just how popular this habit had become in Roman-occupied Gaul. The luxury of heated rooms was naturally appealing but also the whole principle of working up a sweat through sports activities, then relaxing in hot water followed by invigorating cold plunges or baths. These pleasures are still appreciated today by the users of saunas and Turkish baths.

Apart from the primary reason of keeping clean, people came to the baths to relax, discuss politics or business or more usually simply to meet others. Mixed bathing was usually frowned upon, though occasionally tolerated. Generally the baths were open to women in the morning and men in the afternoon.
No evidence has survived of how the baths were really run at Chassenon but their function was probably linked to ritual practices carried out at the temple shrine.

The two hot-water pools viewed from the north-west.

Baths and Religious Centre

Activities at Chassenon Roman baths were therefore not exclusively devoted to personal hygiene, social relations or leisure, nor were the baths strictly speaking a normal public bathing complex serving an urban community. Closely associated with Montélu temple and the other two smaller temples on the site, pilgrims and worshippers came to the baths seeking a cure or for ritual purification in the water prior to religious ceremonies. Chemical and clinical analysis of the springs around the baths show no particular therapeutic value in the water itself. Examination of the site however, provides clues that may point to a significant religious use of the baths in addition to normal bathing. Firstly, there is the question of water supply: Initial hypotheses suspected the main aqueduct as the most likely route of water directly to the baths, but the discovery of a dense array of cisterns or reservoir structures situated on one half of the Montélu temple esplanade may suggest that water was deliberately stored in close proximity to the shrine in the belief it would be imbued with some of the mystical healing properties of the deity worshipped at the temple before being finally channelled to the baths.

Secondly, many ceramic sculptures found at *Cassinomagus* are clearly votive offerings for the cure of illness. Among them can be seen a curious head with four eyes, so depicted not through any lack of skill on the sculptor's part but probably as an invocation of divine aid in curing an eye condition. Another statue found on the site was a terracotta portrait of a person with their arm in a sling, no doubt illustrating the plight of its owner, hoping for a cure at the baths.

Limestone head depicting bearded man with four eyes.

Ceramic *ex-voto* figure with arm in a sling.

Lastly, the building of such unusually large hot pools at *Cassinomagus* was surely no accident and it has been surmised that one of the specialities of the baths was treating rheumatic disorders.

Ceramic statuettes of mother goddess figures found within the bath buildings could imply that religious ceremonies were actually carried out inside the baths. A number of other statues possibly representing Roman gods were also discovered here, including for example a limestone carving of a youth's torso, traditionally identified as the fragment of a sculpture of Apollo, as well as a damaged head belonging perhaps to a statue of the god Mercury.

Head from Gallo-Roman mother goddess statue.

Torso from a limestone statue possibly depicting Apollo.

Current public entrance to Chassenon archaeological site and "Great Wall" on eastern side.

VISITING THE BATHS

Modus Operandi for Roman Bathers

Currently over four-fifths of the central bathing complex can be visited, with just the southern gallery and eastern entrance still awaiting excavation. So far, work on the site has uncovered over a hectare (2.5 acres) of the ancient baths.
Much of the architecture is exceptionally well-preserved, the result of lying buried for so long under layers of earth. Certain walls are more than seven meters high and this provides an insight into the three-floored construction of the baths. The lowest floor was occupied by a series of underground sewage and drainage channels which can be seen in the central and eastern areas of the complex. Service staff occupied the next level up, entering directly via the North Courtyard which was on the same ground floor level. Above them, on the first floor, bathers and other public users of the baths circulated from one room to another.
As with other Roman baths, the layout of buildings at Chassenon reflected their intended use. Thus, bathers would be directed around a specific sequence of rooms according to the principle of invigoratingly abrupt changes from hot to cold environments, as described above. The bathing complex was divided into two symetrical halves along an east-west axis

West side of the bath buildings.

and in this respect its structure resembles large-scale Imperial *thermae*, notably those in Rome. Chassenon baths differ however, by adding a second *palaestra** to the eastern half of the building plus two *frigidaria** and a number of other heated rooms. Normally, for purely economical reasons only intermediate chambers were built as symetrical pairs, bathers following a route that led them progressively from outer rooms towards the middle of the complex. However at Chassenon, bathers started their circuit in the centre of the building and gradually worked their way outwards. Having paid a fee to get in, bathers in large establishments like Chassenon baths would head for the changing-rooms *(apodyterium*)* by the eastern entrance where they could leave their clothing. Several options were then available depending on the type of service required; normal bathing with or without sports activities, or else therapy and cures. The sports sequence began by a visit to one of the *palaestrae**, covered sports areas for gymnastic exercises, boxing or other warm-up activities. Next, dirt and sweat were scraped off the bather's skin with a *strigil** before rubbing down with oil in the *destrictarium**. From there, bathers moved on to the cold room *(frigidarium*)* plunging into its small pool *(alveus*)*. Athletic bathers then crossed paths with ordinary users of the baths in the warm central room *(tepidarium*)*. Carrying towels and perhaps even soap, they would have worn thick-soled sandals provided in the heated

North-eastern corner of north esplanade, with original staff doorway.

Frigidarium viewed from southern open-air *palaestra*.

vestibule to protect their feet from the hot floors in the rooms further along. Any bathers seeking curative treatments would have turned left, to the south, where they could relax in two large hot water pools. Normal users of the baths set off in the opposite direction, first spending time in the hot, dry *sudatio** or sweat-room before moving on to the stiflingly hot and humid *caldarium** room. Here they would plunge into a pool of hot water, occasionally refreshing themselves by splashing cold water over their faces and necks from a *labrum** basin situated in an alcove on the west side of the room. Bathers then proceeded to wash (oil and scrape) in an intermediate, relatively warm *tepidarium** room finally finishing either in the cold water *frigidarium** pool, or going for a swim outdoors in the *natatio** pool. Once dry and after being massaged, fragrant oils bought at the *elaeothesium** (bath centre shop) could be applied if wished in a special annointing room called the *unctorium**. Before dressing again, many bathers soaked up the sun in the *solarium**, a covered outside gallery in either one of the two outer *palaestra** areas. Meanwhile, below them, on the ground floor, a hidden army of specialised staff busily stoked furnaces with wood, cleaned hearths and stored ashes, checked water levels and temperatures of pools, controlled and adjusted water flow to and from boilers using valves and taps. As evening fell, the bath workers would light lamps, clean rooms, change the water in the pools, close shutters over the windows to keep the heat in and open sluice gates to wash out the *latrines**.

Fragment of a bronze boiler found in one of the furnace yards.

First-Floor Public Area of the Baths

The following is a guide to the Chassenon site as it exists today, described in the order a Roman bather would have taken when visiting the baths.

Entrance

The main eastern entrance to the complex has not yet been excavated. Its halls and cloakrooms remain hidden beneath neighbouring fields and under the tarmac of the road to Longeas. However, sloping ground in this part of the site clearly indicates the presence of a monumental flight of steps which would have led up towards the bathing complex entrance gateway.

Upward slope towards entrance, viewed from fields to the east.

Covered *palaestrae**

After changing, all bathers including those seeking cures entered one of two covered *palaestrae** or sports halls, each approximately 17 x 22 m in size. Although excavation of the area is incomplete, work so

Western wall of the southern covered *palaestra* and doorway into *destrictarium/unctorium* chamber.

far has revealed that the north-eastern *palaestra* flooring was supported on wooden beams sprung from large stone blocks barely visible nowadays. Nothing remains of the wall decorations. They were almost certainly divided into three distinct zones one above the other, each register separated by reddish brown bands on a white background. The lowest zone was a painted representation of marble panelling interspersed with plant motifs. Decorative patterns and portraits framed in painted yellow borders occupied the middle zone and a frieze of plant and flower garlands ran along the top of the wall.

Initial cleaning and application of oils

Users not wishing to practise a sport in the *palaestra* proceeded directly to the first heated hall or vestibule where they could begin washing. The 7 x 10 m room was built over a *hypocaust** which as can be seen, has now collapsed. Soundings carried out in 1995 established how the limestone flagstones of the vestibule had been set in a bed of mortar on the *suspensura** floor over the *hypocaust*. Several *tubuli** used to channel heat up the walls, can be seen on the room's south wall. Hot air came to the room from a

South *destrictarium/unctorium* chamber with view of hypocaust *pilae*.

furnace situated in the east courtyard, which although currently inaccessible to visitors may be glimpsed from the road outside. Having worked up a sweat in the *palaestrae*, athletic bathers could then immediately be cleaned in one of two heated *destrictaria/unctoria** rooms, each 10 x 11.5m in size and built directly over a *hypocaust*. Modern installations in the northern room prevent a proper appreciation of its architecture but the structure of the southern *destrictarium/unctorium* is clearly visible with its floor supported from underneath by the brick pillars (*pilae**) of the *hypocaust*. Furnaces situated to the west on the floor below supplied hot air to these intermediate rooms. From here, bathers passed through doors in the western wall to reach the central *tepidarium**.

Main *tepidarium**

This 23 x 10 m hall is the largest single space in the baths complex and lies at its very centre. Two fireplaces built into the northern wall provided heat whilst light came from six large windows whose bases can still be seen in the north and south walls. No doubt the central *tepidarium* was a most pleasant place to meet and chat before continuing treatment or washing at the baths.

South *destrictarium/unctorium*; detail of hypocaust and east *praefurnium* furnace opening.

*Sudatio**

Doors on the right (now permanently obstructed), at the far end of the *tepidarium* led to the *sudatio** or *laconicum** for bathers seeking a hot sauna or sweat bath. This first room, 11 x 16 m in size was never fully cleared during excavations in the mid-twentieth century. Its present state therefore gives a good idea of the amount of earth that had to be removed elsewhere by workers during this period. The several large blocks of carved granite lying on the ground probably came from pillars that once flanked doorways to neighbouring rooms.

*Caldarium**

Two doorways provided access to the *caldarium**, the hottest room in the baths. It was identical in size to the *sudatio* and similarly built over a *hypocaust**.
The south-eastern corner has been fully excavated, revealing how hot air from the north courtyard furnace entered the underfloor space through a hole in the wall and

Caldarium with view of hypocaust *pilae* and *praefurnium* opening.

circulated between the brick *pilae** supporting the weight of the room's floor. On one side, a rectangular opening enabled staff to enter from the furnace courtyard. Temperatures here must have reached at least 45 °C (113 °F), far too hot to walk on the limestone floor without the protection of wooden-soled sandals.

Built into the western wall, a rectangular *alcove** with disturbed ground at its base was previously thought to be a space for *latrines**. However the alcove undoubtedly contained a *labrum**, a type of low basin containing cold water which could be used to refresh occupants of the *caldarium*.

Hot-water *caldarium* pool showing floor of its underlying hypocaust and *praefurnium* opening.

Gutter/rainwater drainage channel around edge of north esplanade and external furnace used to supply hot water to the *caldarium* pool.

An *alveus**, or hot-water bathing pool built on a rubble base can be seen by the north wall. Three steps still visible today, led bathers down into the water which was one metre deep and heated in boilers situated just off the north courtyard. The hot water travelled along pipes cut into the western wall, traces of their passage still being visible low down near the ground. A *hypocaust* receiving hot air from an external furnace in the north courtyard, kept the water hot on its journey to the pool.

North intermediate *tepidarium**

After transpiring for a while in the hot *caldarium*, bathers left the room by a small eastern door and entered the northern *tepidarium**, a 10 x 4 m area where they were massaged and had oil rubbed into their skin. Once lit by three windows, little has survived of this room.

The remains of hypocaust *pilae* can clearly be viewed from the wooden walkway and we know the room was heated by a furnace to the south, on the ground floor below. Marks on the floor left by a mason's line as it was plucked and touched the fresh mortar, show us that the mason tried twice before he managed to get a satisfactory straight line, intended as a guide to aligning the brick *pilae* in a regularly-spaced grid pattern.

Flagstones covering central drainage channel seen from *tepidarium* footbridge.

North *frigidarium**

Washed and warm, bathers next proceeded to a large cold room, the *frigidarium*, 13.5 x 17 m in size and lit by three windows. Here they plunged into a cold water pool or *alveus**. Today it bears little resemblance to its original form. The tops of understructure vaults visible nowadays were only revealed when the north-west corner collapsed at some point in the 19th century. In Roman times however, limestone paving stones would have continued to the northern wall which like all the others in the room had a mortar facing coated with white paint.

The cold plunge pool itself, the final stage in the Roman sauna process, has completely disappeared as has its underlying rubble banking. All that remains is a small triangular opening near ground level, just under the eastern window, identified as a overflow drainage channel which also served to evacuate water when the pool was being cleaned.

North *palaestra** and *natatio**

Although visitors currently enter the site here, this is where Roman bathers would have ended their journey through the baths. They left the *frigidarium** by a doorway in its north-eastern corner and when the weather was fine, could take a dip in the large open-air swimming pool (*natatio**). The outline of its rim is still visible together with an overflow drain in the north-west corner.
Summer bathers would have also used the space as a *solarium**, sheltered around its edges by an L-shaped colonnaded gallery. The latter, like the northern gallery is now invisible, either destroyed or lying partially buried under the nearby road.

Hot pools

Southern hot-water pool; detail of steps and bottom of pool.

An original feature of Chassenon is the presence of two large hot-water pools. Access was via a doorway on the left at the far end of the central *tepidarium**, the pools occupying two adjacent warm rooms where bathers could pass from one to the other through three openings or bays, flanked by pillars made from large blocks of granite. The pillars still bear traces of the hooks used to attach their decorative veneers.
Each pool is approximately 15 m long, 10 m wide and almost 1,4 m in depth, deep enough for the immersion of bathers as part of some form of therapeutic treatment. The pool bottoms were lined with limestone slabs most of which have

Southern hot-water pool; west alcove showing a section of the overflow channel.

disappeared, with just the impressions of their forms remaining in the mortar. A series of steps led bathers down into the water from the pool margin and although the stone edging no longer exists, the current wooden walkway for visitors occupies the same area and so gives an idea of the pools' original appearance. As you move around the pools, two benches can be seen built on the north wall while on the western side, the original Roman window openings are still extant.
A rectangular *alcove** on the west wall of the southern pool room marks the site of a small *labrum**, or cold-water basin. Remains of paving can be seen on the ground here, as well as the remains of a deep drainage channel designed to receive water overflowing from the pool. This demonstrates how careful Roman architects were in controlling the circulation of water. In the southern wall, a recess is fitted with three benches.

Southern hot-water pool; benches built into south-side wall.

Water for the pools was heated in boilers over fires in the furnace courtyard just to the east. It flowed into the pools through small quadrangular orifices in the eastern wall. Each evening, water was drained by opening plugs in the north-western corners of the pools, from where it flowed into a waste channel running along the outside of the west face of the bath buildings.
Temperature of air and water in the rooms was kept high through added heat from the *hypocaust** system. Here however,

Northern hot-water pool with impressions of paving slabs, part of western wall and drainage plughole.

instead of suspended floors over *pilae**, the hypocaust consisted of a network of channels crossing and surrounding the pools' foundations, as can clearly be seen in the south pool.

Southern hot-water pool with view of hypocaust channel running under the pool.

South *frigidarium** and *palaestrae**

Similarly to bathers who left the hot rooms via a *tepidarium* on the north side of the building, those who had received treatment in the two hot pools on the south side next passed through an intermediary warm *tepidarium** where they were rubbed down with oils. Inaccessible today, the room contains only a few remnants of the hypocaust* system that was once fed from the south furnace courtyard.

Users of the baths then moved through to the large *frigidarium** cold room, almost identical in every detail to the one on the northern side of the building. Standing in the north-west corner we have to imagine this broad space entirely covered with a roof, the room's floor and lower walls paved or lined with limestone slabs.

Among the many openings in the walls, there is one that looks out onto the southern furnace courtyard. Despite a metal staircase that descends nowadays to the lower floor levels of the building, this opening was not originally a doorway at all but in fact a 3.4 metre-wide window which must have more than amply illuminated the room.

A small cold pool lies along the southern wall of the *frigidarium** with its paving slabs fully restored. After a quick dip in this cold pool, users would have then dried themselves and been rubbed with oils in the south *unctorium**.

Southern *frigidarium* with view of paving and wall facings.

Cold-water pool in southern *frigidarium*.

A large doorway almost 5 metres wide in the south-west wall of the *frigidarium* opens onto a spacious southern courtyard and although the area has still to be excavated, it seems probable it was used for sports and exercising as well as for relaxing in the sun during summertime. When the weather was good, a south-eastern doorway on the opposite wall allowed bathers to leave the *frigidarium* and go for a swim in the *natatio** in the porticoed *palaestra** area.

Southern *palaestra* with its *natatio* swimming pool during excavations in the 1970s.

Southern *palaestra* with *breccia* paving stones and manhole to inspect east-side drainage channel.

Although the swimming pool is currently filled in, the fine workmanship of its surrounding paving made from local meteorite-impact stone, can still be admired. Near the north-western doorway a cavity can be seen in the ground which was used by maintenance staff to enter the eastern underground sewer. The latter channelled water from the south *frigidarium** pool and outdoors *natationes** pools to an exit point sixty metres away, in the north forecourt or esplanade.

Galleries and adjoining rooms

Two long, straight galleries sixty metres in length, completed the bathing complex to the north and south. They are currently being excavated and therefore cannot normally be visited. Indeed, their function remains unknown for the present, though preliminary evidence shows that the southern gallery had a floor made of ash wood. Although the north gallery upper floor and ground floor have completely disappeared, it is known they were the same height as the southern gallery, in other words, six meters above their present level.

North furnace yard staircase to *praefurnia* on west side.

Electromagnetic surveys* show that both galleries terminated at their western ends with square towers approximately thirteen metres wide. Hopefully, excavations in the near future will elucidate their exact functions but in the meantime, results indicate that the south-west tower probably housed a reservoir stocking water for the baths, being directly supplied itself via an aqueduct from the temple's array of cisterns. Since the north-west tower is located over a waste water drain, it may possibly have housed the baths' public *latrines**.

Ground Floor and Service Areas

Only service staff had access to the ground floor area. There simply was no passage-way to connect the public first floor levels with the lower part of the building. The modern stairway running between the north-east *palaestra** (with its *natatio*) and the north courtyard, goes through the walls of the gallery itself. In addition, during Roman times some of the rooms on the ground floor were totally inaccessible even to staff.

Collapsed substructure vaults under northern *frigidarium* floor.

Wall of substructure chamber with marks of masons' trowels from Roman times.

Barrel vault covered with modern graffiti in substructure chamber.

Vaults

Sixteen vaulted rooms of this type have been discovered so far, all perfectly preserved in every detail. Their function was to compensate for the sloping ground and so provide a level platform for the public baths above. A clear view of the technique and its realisation can be seen under the north *frigidarium** where two of the vaults have partially collapsed.
These closed spaces have been left undisturbed for centuries and are virtually as new. Mortar on the ceiling still bears the imprint of planks used to form the shape of the vaults whilst on the walls, marks left by the triangular trowels of Roman masons are also visible.
Built in groups of three or four, the rooms had diagonal connecting passages between them at the time of their construction. This arrangement not only facilitated the movement of workmen but also aided drainage of leaks from above. Starting at the north *frigidarium**, it is possible to enter several of these rooms which since the 19th century have often had visitors and were even used as hideouts during the Second World War. Proof of this can be seen in the abundant *graffiti* covering

the walls with names of local families from Longeas and Chassenon. In modern times, a passageway was bored through the walls of vaults beneath the *caldarium* and *sudatio*, so creating space for a modest Chassenon Baths museum. Similarly, during 19th century excavations, a tunnel was dug between one of these rooms and an adjoining vault used to stock ashes, thus opening up access to visitors and excavators. It therefore should not be confused with the original arrangement of this area in Roman times, when staff could only enter a single storeroom plus two vaulted zones used for stocking ashes produced by the bath furnaces.

Ash storage chamber opened in modern times to provide access to west-side rooms.

North Esplanade

Staff entered the baths through the north gallery. A large doorway built into the eastern wall allowed goods, logs and other general materials to be delivered directly to the service level and stored in a 90m^2 space below the gallery itself.
Two sets of successive doors brought bath workers out onto the north esplanade, an area 1000m^2 in size, around whose edges a circuit of drains collected water running off the

View of relieving arch and vaulted east drainage channel seen from north esplanade.

surrounding roofs. On the eastern side of this space, the vaulted top of an underground outflow channel can be spotted, designed to drain water from the cold-water pools in the eastern half of the first-floor level above.

To the south-west can be seen the only outdoors *praefurnium** in the baths complex. It was built over the flagstones of the peripheral gutter and served to heat water for the small basin (*alveus**) in the *caldarium**.

Following the flagstones that cover the main drain leads directly into the heart of the baths complex.

Furnace yard entrance gateway from the north esplanade.

Store Room

Ground floor storeroom doorway.

This is the only vaulted room in the service sector of the baths to have had a door, as shown by the bearing shaft hole drilled into the first step of its flight of stairs. It was an easily accessible space, measuring 7.3 x 3 metres, probably used to store tools for maintenance work, or even perhaps more valuable products used by bathers such as oils and perfumes.

North Furnace Yard

The north furnace yard, situated just beyond the store room is a 180 m^2 space that was originally partly covered with roofing. Six *praefurnia** were situated here. The space is also crossed by the baths main drainage channel, cut directly into the impact *breccia** rock of its ground.

North furnace yard, viewed from north-west.

Steps leading to the hearths of two furnaces can be seen on the east side of the courtyard. The furnaces heated air for hypocaust* systems supplying the north *destrictarium / unctorium** room as well as the large central *tepidarium** hall on the public level one floor above.

On the opposite side of the courtyard, to the west, large blocks of *breccia** rock form a series of steps down to a well-defined area which housed a group of four *praefurnia** which could be reached through three large bay openings.

The two smaller furnaces to the left and right supplied hot air to the central *tepidarium**, and also to the north intermediate *tepidarium**. The two larger central furnaces, whose hearths and hot

North furnace yard, looking towards the west-side *praefurnia* beyond the central platform.

North-west corner of north furnace yard with the *praefurnium* responsible for heating the *caldarium*.

air channels may easily be observed, fed the *sudatio** and *caldarium** room *hypocausts**. Heating was therefore a simple process of lighting a fire in the furnace hearth so producing hot air that was then drawn up and along channels until it reached the underfloor hypocaust system of a nearby room.

The northernmost hearth still has the remains of iron legs belonging to a grille that was placed above the hearth. This served as a support for a large bronze boiler in which water was heated before being piped into the *caldarium** hot pool. A short section of a terracotta duct can be seen on the last step of the side stairs. It served either as sheathing for lead pipes or maybe as an overflow conduit. Hot water left the boiler along lead pipes, crossing the north wall inside a rectangular shaft whose opening is still visible.

North furnace yard with view of the *tepidarium* furnace and water duct built through wall.

An overall eye could be kept on the furnaces and heating system from the raised terrace between the two hearths and in addition, from this vantage point, staff in neighbouring rooms could be contacted via rectangular openings in the west wall when the temperature of water or air elsewhere in the building needed checking.

Ash Store Rooms

The southern furnace yard can be reached by following a corridor that is paved with *breccia** rock flagstones laid over the central main drain. On either side of the corridor are a total of six rooms that have been perfectly preserved since Roman times. As with the other structural supporting spaces described above, they provide us with a pristine illustration of the techniques used in their construction.

Groundfloor central corridor.

Numerous traces left in the mortar by trowels and the imprint of coffering boards bear witness to those who built the baths. Occasionally letters and symbols can be seen, moulded in relief from marks made by workmen on the

planks they pressed into the wet mortar. Abundant Gallo-Roman graffiti adorns the ceiling though much of it is indecipherable.
Unlike the vaulted spaces described above which were sealed off in Roman times, these rooms functioned as dumps for ashes produced by the furnaces. Indeed, you walk today on several dozen centimetres of ashes and coal in this part of the baths complex, layers built up over time as the workers dumped furnace ashes here at the end of every day. Once cool, they were retrieved to be recycled or sold elsewhere.

Worker's mark in the mortar of one of the substructure chambers.

Ash storage room doorways.

Study of charcoal found on this level of the baths complex confirms that the principal fuel was logged wood coming from a number of different local tree varieties. These mainly included oak, beech and alder, but also buckthorn, hornbeam, dogwood, common maple, holly, hazel, hawthorn, poplar, apple, pear, willow, elder and lime. Such results give an insight into the management and supply of fuel sources to keep the baths working and incidentally also provide proof that Chassenon never lacked firewood at any time in its history.

South Furnace Yard

The layout of this second courtyard is similar to the north furnace yard, except here there are only four *praefurnia* instead of six.

On the eastern side, the restored remains of a flight of steps lead to the *praefurnium** responsible for heating the south *destrictarium*/unctorium** *hypocaust** system. It was probably protected from rain by a wooden canopy or roofing. A deep vertical gash in the eastern wall indicates the location of a main water supply pipe, lending weight to the hypothesis that this furnace as well as the others here served to heat water for bathing pools.

The courtyard was split in two towards the west by a stone wall with three openings, on the other side of which stood the remaining three furnaces. The smallest *praefurnium**, on the south side, heated a *hypocaust* travelling under the intermediate *tepidarium**. The two other furnaces, both large and similar in construction to those in the north furnace yard, are separated by a high platform or terrace that can be reached by climbing a central staircase. Both heated the hypocaust system and hot water supply to the pools closest at

South furnace yard with view of west-side *praefurnia* and central platform.

South furnace yard showing *praefurnium* used for heating *destrictarium/unctorium*.

hand. Openings in the western wall provide a clue as to how water was able to transit from boilers to pools, the larger cavities next to them being designed to facilitate communication between rooms. Again, grooves running vertically up the north wall indicate part of the route taken by pipes feeding water to the boilers.
A drainage outlet near the foot of the south wall is connected to the water storage tank in the room next door.

Vertical mark of water pipe in south furnace yard wall.

"Cistern"

The closed vaulted space to the south of the courtyard served as a reservoir collecting water running off the roofs as well as infiltrations and seepages. It was therefore linked to the gutters in the southern half of the building. Water collected in this manner, then either flowed out into the centre of the south furnace yard or passed under the west-wall furnaces and from there, joined the central drain. Water from the reservoir was not intended for use in pools but instead was used to help extinguish fires that might break out in the yard. This fire prevention system proved to be ultimately insufficient when, two centuries after its construction, the Roman baths burned down a first time.

Glossary

Alcove: recess in a wall or rectangular outward projection of a wall.

Alveus: small hot or cold water basin.

Apodyterium: changing room or cloakroom.

Breccia: a type of metamorphic rock formed from conglomeration of mineral elements bonded together by a natural cement. The type of rock around Chassenon is known as *impact breccia* since it is the result of a massive geological disturbance caused by the impact of a giant meteor in this region.

Caldarium: the hottest room in the Roman baths (either dry or humid heat) with basins and sometimes a bathing pool of hot water.

Cella: literally a "room" for a deity, the inner sanctum of a temple.

Destrictarium: heated room where an implement called a *strigil** was used to scrape the bather's skin clean.

Elaeothesium: shop selling oils and perfumes.

Exhedra: rectangular or semicircular space projecting out of a room, normally furnished with benches and on a portico.

Electromagnetic survey: method using electrical waves to detect slight changes in magnetic fields caused by the presence of masonry structures hidden below ground.

Fanum: a type of Roman temple with a central space and peripheral gallery, typical of Gaul under Roman domination.

Frigidarium: cold room with basin of cold water and sometimes a shower too.

Hypocaust: underfloor heating system.

Labrum: cold water basin either continuously supplied with water or not.

Laconicum: see *sudatio*.

Latrines: public toilets.

Natatio: open air cold-water swimming pool located in the *palaestra*.

Opus caementicium: Roman concrete made from lime mortar and stone fragments.

Opus vittatum: facing of wall using regularly arranged small rectangular blocks.

Opus vittatum mixtum: as above but with alternating courses of rectangular blocks with one or two courses of brick. Sometimes called block-and-brick technique.

Palaestra: indoors or outside sports area.

Peutinger's Tabula (or Table): medieval copy of a map of routes and roads under the Roman Empire.

Praefurnium: furnace supplying heat to a hypocaust system. Usually also equipped with a stand for a boiler to produce hot water.

Solarium: uncovered sunbathing area generally in a *palaestra* or open courtyard

Strigil: curved metallic scraper to clean and massage the body.

Sudatio: hot room or sweat bath room without a pool or basin.

Suspensura: principal component of a hypocaust system consisting of the floor of a heated room held up on an array of brick pillars.

Tepidarium: warm room heated by a hypocaust.

Tubuli: bundles of interconnected terracotta tubes carrying hot air from the hypocaust up the walls of heated rooms.

Unctorium: warm room where oil could be applied to the skin before or after bathing.

Viguery: Medieval secular administrative region (*viguerie* in French) overseen by an officer called a *viguier*.